Mary McLeod Bethune

A LIFE OF RESOURCEFULNESS

by Kristin Sterling

PULL AHEAD BOOKS
Biographies

Lerner Publications Company • Minneapolis

Photo Acknowledgments

The photographs in this book are reproduced with the permission of: Florida State Archives, pp. 4, 6, 8, 10, 12, 13, 14, 15, 16, 18, 19, 20, 21, 25; Library of Congress (LC-USZ62-78481), p. 9; © Hulton Archive/Getty Images, p. 22; © Bettmann/CORBIS, p. 24; © Gordon Parks/Hulton Archive/Getty Images, p. 26.

Front cover: Florida State Archives

Lerner Publications Company
A division of Lerner Publishing Group, Inc.
241 First Avenue North
Minneapolis, MN 55401 U.S.A.

Website address: www.lernerbooks.com

Words in **bold type** are explained in a glossary on page 31.

Library of Congress Cataloging-in-Publication Data

Sterling, Kristin.
    Mary McLeod Bethune : a life of resourcefulness / by Kristin Sterling.
        p. cm. — (Pull ahead books. Biographies)
    Includes index.
    ISBN 978-0-8225-8588-6 (lib. bdg. : alk. paper) 1. Bethune, Mary McLeod, 1875-1955—Juvenile literature. 2. Resourcefulness—Juvenile literature. 3. African American women political activists—Biography—Juvenile literature. 4. African American women educators—Biography—Juvenile literature. 5. African American women social reformers—Biography—Juvenile literature. 6. African Americans—Biography—Juvenile literature. 7. African Americans—Civil rights—History—20th century—Juvenile literature. I. Title.
    E185.97.B34S74 2008
    370.92--dc22 [B]   2007025131

Manufactured in the United States of America
1 2 3 4 5 6 – JR – 13 12 11 10 09 08

Table of Contents

Mary McLeod Bethune in the early 1900s

No Ink?

Mary McLeod Bethune had a problem. Her students did not have any ink for their pens! Mary crushed berries, and her students wrote with the juice. Mary was good at finding ways to solve problems. Her **resourcefulness** made her a famous teacher and leader.

Mary was born in this cabin in South Carolina. Her sisters, Rachel and Maria, stand in front of the cabin.

A Resourceful Student

Mary McLeod was born in South Carolina in 1875. She was the fifteenth child in her family. Her parents had been slaves.

Mary was the first person in her family to go to school. She went to a school for **African American** children.

Mary's parents, Samuel and Patsy McIntosh McLeod

Mary went to a school like this one.

Mary was a very good student. She knew education would help her have a better life.

Mary as a young woman

A Resourceful Teacher

Mary went to **college**. Then she became a teacher. There were not many schools for African Americans at that time. Mary started her own school for African American girls.

Mary was a good teacher.

Mary started the school in a little house. Five young girls were her only students.

Mary did not have money to buy supplies. Her students used boxes for desks.

Mary's school grew quickly.

Mary worked hard to raise money for the school. She planned concerts and held bake sales.

Students learn how to do laundry.

Mary had to raise money for her school.

She talked to **wealthy** people. Some people were mean to her. Others gave her money for the school.

Mary had to get more space for her school.

A Resourceful Leader

Mary could do a lot with a little. She did not waste money or **resources**. She used them to make her school a better place.

Mary's school changed over the years.
It started with classes for young girls.

These students are learning sewing and needlework.

These students are in a cooking class.

Mary's students got older. She added high school classes. She also added job training programs.

This school building is called Faith Hall.

In 1923, Mary's school combined with Cookman Institute. This was a college for men. The new school was named Bethune-Cookman College.

Mary was the president of the college.

Mary was a good college president.

Mary in front of the U.S. Capitol

Mary Takes a Stand

Mary thought all people should have the **right** to learn. At this time, black people did not have the same rights as white people. For example, many black children could not go to the same schools as white children. Mary wanted to help solve this problem.

Mary talked to big groups of people about equal rights for black people. She even talked to the president of the United States!

Mary speaks about equal rights to a huge crowd of people.

First Lady Eleanor Roosevelt *(left)* visits Mary's college.

President Franklin Roosevelt asked
Mary to lead a program for African
American teenagers and young adults.
She helped them to find good jobs.

Mary works in her office.

A Life of Resourcefulness

Mary was a resourceful person. She was good at finding ways to solve problems. She was able to make life better for many African Americans.

MARY McLEOD BETHUNE TIMELINE

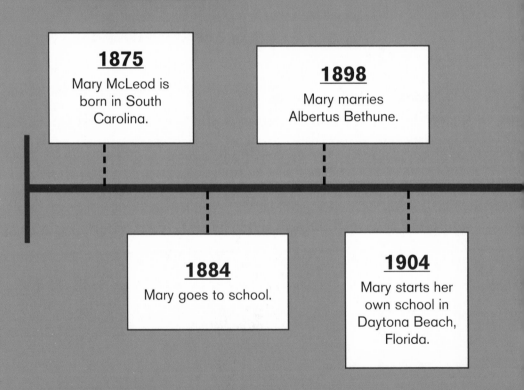

1875
Mary McLeod is born in South Carolina.

1898
Mary marries Albertus Bethune.

1884
Mary goes to school.

1904
Mary starts her own school in Daytona Beach, Florida.

1923
Mary's school becomes Bethune-Cookman College.

1955
Mary dies of a heart attack.

1936
Mary begins working for a government agency to help young black people.

More about Mary McLeod Bethune

● Mary had one son, Albert. He was also a teacher.

● In 1935, Mary was honored with the Spingarn Medal. The National Association for the Advancement of Colored People (NAACP) awards it for outstanding achievement by a black American.

● In 1985, a postage stamp was made honoring Mary McLeod Bethune.

Websites

Better World Heroes
http://betterworldheroes.com/bethune.htm

The Florida Memory Project
http://www.floridamemory.com/OnlineClassroom/
MaryBethune/photo_page1.cfm

White House Dream Team
http://www.whitehouse.gov/kids/dreamteam/
marybethune.html

Glossary

African American: an American who has African ancestors

college: a school people can go to after high school

resourcefulness: the ability to deal with hard situations and solve problems

resources: something that can be used for support or help

right: the power to do something

wealthy: rich, having a lot of money

Index